PRIVATE PARTS

PRIVATE PARTS

Fiona Pitt-Kethley

Chatto & Windus   LONDON

Published in 1987 by
Chatto & Windus Ltd
30 Bedford Square
London WC1B 3RP

Second impression 1988

British Library Cataloguing in Publication Data
Pitt-Kethley, Fiona
    Private parts.
    I. Title
    821'.914   PR6066.I7/

ISBN 0-7011-3206-X

Some of the poems first appeared in the following:
*London Review of Books, New Statesman, Observer, Encounter, Times
Literary Supplement, 2 Plus 2, Anglo-Welsh Review, Gown* and *New
Departures.*

'Charity' was a prizewinner in the 1984 National Poetry Competition.

Printed in Great Britain by
Redwood Burn Ltd
Trowbridge, Wiltshire

Contents

Gala Day

'Gala Day' on the Hastings–Tonbridge line
was all 'special attractions and displays . . .
50p per person (Adult or Child)'.
They'd painted stations right along the way
and hung out plastic flags – red, white and blue.
The programme had a picture on the back –
The Wrotham White Star Sword Dance Team at work –
six knickerbockered blokes with left legs raised;
the youngest had bagpipes under one arm;
the fattest held a pentacle of swords;
they all had beards, bow-ties and cummerbunds.

A harassed beauty queen came round the train
with pencils, beer-mats, biros, stickers, bags
and 'twirly hats'. I got a bag and pen.
The trains were packed with Mums and Dads and kids.
('Look Dad, you can get in half-price with this
to Hastings Castle and the Caves.' Dad sat
on Mummy's lap and said, 'They'd have to pay
to get *me* to go round that lot.')

I didn't see a lot that day myself.
I somehow missed the Sunoak Ladies' Clog Dance Team.
I didn't hear 'Sussex Brass' silver band,
or take the vintage bus at Etchingham
for Bodiam Castle's armour videos,
or get a discount at Kentucky Fried.

I just stopped off in Tunbridge Wells for wine –
Lamberhurst Vineyards gave free tastings there –
then thought I'd try some village pub for lunch.
I got the train and looked for likely stops.

First, I tried Frant – or rather Bells Yew Green,
which has no bells, no yew and little green.

(Frant I discovered was a winding mile uphill
and out of sight – an English signpost mile.
The Brecknock Arms did not do food, they said.)

Back to the train. A stop or two away
I managed to get a Stilton Ploughman's Lunch.
The landlady looked fat and deaf and mad;
the barman left his beerpulls run and run;
there were a thousand trippers at the door:

My last stop off was for a country church –
the finest in the county, someone said –
a fourteenth-century one with a small tower,
verdigrised Xs bolted through all sides.
I bought a notelet in the porch, I don't
know why – a brass-rubbed lady and two knights –
de Echynghams with piously folded hands
and lions sitting at their pointed feet.
(Richard Goulden B.A. had done the print.)
The envelope was all gummed up with damp.
I stuffed it in my bag and ran across
some muddy graves to catch the waiting train.

Family Planning

A shop in Hastings' George Street sells kits marked
'Yoga For Contraception' on the front.
I've often wondered what the packs contain
and half intend to point a spendthrift friend
at one, next time she visits for the day.
I'm mean – 1.20 seems a lot – perhaps
the box just holds a little slip which says:
Stay in the lotus pose so no man can
get near enough to impregnate.

Just round the corner where the High Street starts,
on every other Thursday, 10–12,
the FPC give out their pills and things.
Two women stand outside to chat and watch.

Inside, nurse, doctor and receptionist
sit sipping instant from blue and white mugs
stamped with pill brand names, male and female signs.
The posters advertise chiropody,
sensitive teeth, pregnancy and VD.
Trade's usually quite slow.

Once, a young mum with two kids running round,
told all she'd had no bother since her coil
had been 'installed' ten years or so ago.
Her children found a duck in grey chewed foam
buried beneath the pile of *Woman's Own*
and rammed it in her mouth.

When the whole roomful had been weighed in turn,
all the blood pressures and cycles noted,
the tri-annual smears taken, the breasts felt,
all side-effects duly recorded
and supplies passed out to the wise non-virgins,

an old, old lady sitting there, brought out her card.
People just sort of looked at her askance.
'The eighth, 11.45,' she said.
'The eighth's next week.' They told her where she was.
'I thought it was the day for feet,' she groaned.

Ghost Train

I flirted with horror on ghost trains,
relishing the caresses of cobwebs,
laughing through electronic screams.

How individual each man's view of fear –
the plastic skeletons at every turn,
lions painted on double swinging doors,
(once even, a plastic girl in bra and pants,
a skull beneath her wig when she swung round).

The catharsis of terror is over
so quickly – not spun out like life. You come
to light from darkness, walk even ground
after the Crazy House's corridors
and tilted spongy floors.

Tastes

'Is *The Duchess of Malfi* miserable?'
a friend who's good at getting cheap seats asked.
'It is,' I said. 'I'd like to see it though.'
'How many die?' 'Oh, almost everyone . . .'

We went last week. She pissed off at half time
to a piano bar in Marble Arch.
(She'd wangled us into the Green Room first.
We'd had some Guinnesses and that had made
her restless she explained; she had to go;
another time she might have liked the play.)

I heard two students in the row behind
discuss things at the end. 'Bosola wasn't
entirely a baddie, I suppose?'
'I don't know,' the friend said. 'I've got some notes
on it at home but can't remember them.'

After the show I went back to King's Cross –
I was to stay the night at my friend's place.
I had her key in case she rolled in late.
She did, after three brandies and two Macks,
and told me which Novello songs she'd sung.

'What happened in the play?' she asked. 'Who died?'
I had to give a blow by blow account
before the talk went on to men and kicks
she'd had with butter, ice-cream, eggs.

She offered me *The Stud* for my night's read –
she hadn't finished it – 'It's not as good
as *Hollywood Wives*.' Her bed looked sinister
with blood-red sheets beneath a black duvet.

Man, Woman and Superman

We were working in a cold November,
one night at Pinewood, on *Superman II*,
shivering in our thin, summer clothing
as the wind whistled through the open set.
Between the takes, like moths, we huddled to
the fake-warm brightness of the lights. A gust
of rain, and Superman, legs tweely crossed
in tights, et cetera, opened his brolly.
The assistants ran here and there, voices
scrambled impossibly through megaphones,
the two-way radios at their belts gave out
new orders, talking at cross purposes.
Soon after, silence. Some men descended
from scaffolding to blow up brand-new cars
(parts all screwed loose). On pain of dismissal
we kept our faces solemn – not a smile.
The unit's chip-van soon joined in with flames
(unplanned). A dark, unholy incubus
of black, oiled soot wound from its roof before
a dull explosion. Coughing and choking
we crowded the Daily Planet's office.

You don't talk a lot on a noisy job
like that – nor in the rush to cash your chits.
Weeks on, I heard how one man fell that night –
his heart – he'd faked his age to get the call.
The others, laughing, unaware, passed round ·
a photo of a man dubbed 'Supercock'
(twenty-eight inches of it, so they said).
The women speculated on its use –
lovemaking Pyramus-and-Thisbe style –
pictured him trousered from the Isle of Man.
The men, while saying it must be a fake,
still thought that one like that would be most prized.

I class it as an extra's legend
with the one about the fat, old 'crowd artiste'
who wet her costume on the Titanic
and got the sack. (She also, it is said,
pulled up her skirts and showed a rural scene
to some director who'd offended her –
the film was *Dragonslayer*.)

When Superman and all the rest had gone
that night, it's said, a cunning thief crept through
Metropolis, and, opening all the doors,
took the prams out of Mothercare and filled
them full of videos from the other shops.

Laryngitis

I usually shun doctors (for you don't
know where their hands have been – though you can guess;
and surgeries are full of the diseased –
the coughers all have flu and bronchitis,
the scratchers rashes, but the silent ones
worry me most – they could have anything).
Once, struck with a sore throat, I went to one.
I'd overworked my voice – one scream too much.
He told me to shut up for two whole weeks.

And so I was struck dumb – a sore trial
for a woman of my disposition –
reduced to a toneless whisper, I, who
had leant backwards to kiss the Blarney Stone
and could argue the pants off anyone,
dialectically-speaking. (At school
I had a running bet that I could keep
the RK teacher talking every week
on esoteric points of doctrine I'd
cooked up. I even once conspired to make
all the Old Testament prophecies fit
Judas, not Jesus, like a glove.)

A fortnight on, I returned gladly
to my old ways, talking through half the night,
yelling, screaming, belting out high notes,
ventriloquising speeches for my cats,
laughing uproariously. Two weeks of quiet's
enough for anyone. In Writing, though,
the Chirons and Demetriuses who rule
would make of me a dumb Lavinia.

A dissident citizen of the world,
no country opens up its arms to me.
Woman is often rendered silent,
her greatest shout defined as stridency,
the whisper of her presence hardly heard.

Dirty Old Men

Old men, the dirty kind, come in two sorts —
the nice ones and the nasty. They're much like
those who pass by a fruit stall. Some just think
how nice an apple would have been if they'd
had teeth. Others without the wherewithal
to buy or eat, must sink their grimy thumbs
into the nectarines.

On Charing Cross an English wino said:
'You've got charisma . . . just like me.' Elsewhere,
a Polish drunk, stretched happy on a bench,
called me 'A real lady' when I passed
him back the cherry wine he'd dropped. I'd say
these were both nice ones of the dirty type.
Likewise an English master I once knew —
I was to play Titania at his school.
He wished to have the fairies in the show
all starkers, me too, and painted silver.
The governors refused, he settled for
transparent lamé catsuits, Mary Quant.
I had a most uncomfortable time —
Cobweb and Co made me a fakir's bed
with pins. (The sight of me, laddered into
indecency, getting a leg over
poor Bottom made the local vicar blanch —
I was a leading light in his church choir.)

This teacher had a wall at home, filled up
with codpieces he'd made – just for the play.
And most were much too big, for Puck kept all
his Strepsils down his and we heard them roll
with every cartwheel and each somersault.

The other sort – made asses by their own
illusions in the winter of their years,
not hooked on Shakespeare or the bottle's joys,
are not content with dreams, must pry and poke,
place their corpse-withered lips upon your cheek,
their grave-claws on your shoulders. Like old goats,
they chumble and spoil everything they touch,
blaming some Circe for their beastliness.
Decrepit parasites – they'd suck our youth's
blood to prolong their own.

Restored Faith

Men aren't so bad, really, I thought. (The post
was good to me that day and it was fine.)
I went out with an open mind (for once),
and met an old age pensioner. He first
inquired my age, told me I looked it, then
went on to ask if I had many sons.
I ought to procreate, he said, before
it was too late.

It's funny – I can always find a man
capable of restoring all my faith
in male obnoxiousness.

He then went on to try to sell his book –
'A thesis on the economic state
of the Sudan,' he said, 'Harvard UP
and only fourteen pounds.'

'I have to go and get the shopping in,'
I lied. He followed me, block after block,
and told me how he'd stood and watched a pair
of seagulls copulating on the prom.
(He'd timed them too, it seemed.) 'The male bird spent
fifteen or twenty minutes finishing
and then went off, leaving her standing there.
I was so disillusioned that I dropped
into this café here for fish and chips.
Ah, but when I came out that bird was back
feeding her little pieces, beak to beak;
and that restored my faith in love.
'Have you had breakfast, by the way?' he said.
'Or could I offer you something to eat?'

Intruders

In early teens, inspired by Keats (I think),
I had St Agnes' Eve-type fantasies
of handsome strangers merging with my dreams.

One day, I woke to find a tall, black man
in a donkey-jacket and jeans. His looks
were only average. I sat up in bed
and chatted – I thought it safest to pretend
I had mistaken him for the plumber
and tell him where the bathroom was. He looked
at my watch on the mantelpiece, but left
with nothing. The police never caught him.
(One asked if I had 'men friends', though.)
'A dangerous man,' they said.

My visitor was a disappointment –
like blind dates. I had one of those, later,
with a wrong number who'd flattered my voice.
Over a drink, he told me eager tales
about a hostel he had visited.
'I saw a pair in every room,' he said,
'doing a sixty-nine.' It sounded like
an advent calendar.

Rubber Goods

At fourteen, disillusionment set in
when our loved history teacher fell from grace –
we'd all admired her dashing talk at twelve –
something quite new for Haberdashers' Aske's.
One of our number had filled up a slip
to get her a free pack of rubber goods.
BR did not appreciate our gift.
Even the sexually retarded ones
who still had crushes on her were put off.
How pompous, we all thought – why should she mind
a set of condoms coming through the post?
Look, if she didn't want to use the things,
couldn't she toss 'em to the cat, or stick
the packet in a pillar-box?

Each evening handwriting experts went through
our desks, comparing slopes of l's and t's,
narrowing down the suspect list to one –
my friend who'd once done verses for the mag,
'The Errant Knight' containing rhymes like 'suck'
and 'fuck' – unsigned of course. I wonder what
they thought of all our stuff – the lepers' squares
(as if they didn't have enough to bear
without our handiwork); the paper pants
one girl would wear for gym, hoping they'd split.
(A nympho with obliging parents, she
gave snogging parties with the St Paul's boys.)
There also were the books we'd mitigate
the boredom of our lessons with – the big
black one on lesbians I showed to Mum.
She read it through, just muttering 'Well!' The friend
who'd nicked it from her father's surgery
was frightened when she heard, and passing by

my house each day would walk like Groucho Marx
and keep unseen below the privet hedge.
What did the searchers make of that long screed
one girl received by answering an ad
in *Time Out*'s columns. There were nine pages.
The writer boasted 'draws of rubber goods'.

Those 'experts' never really got it right.
Against all evidence, it was a last
small fling by one quiet, academic girl –
pigtailed and spectacled. We'd once been friends
in mischief and would somersault or hang
on Ealing's bus shelters, turned upside down,
our satchels spilling on the ground. We were
too dull to take them off. The school had wiped
the fun from her, all but that last small spark.

Fan Letter

'Geoff is the name and lust's my game' . . .
I've had a fan letter from 'Geoffrey X'.
He's even given me his home address.
(Mum says Roath Park in Cardiff's the posh end
of town.) Geoff lets me know that 'dreadful men
are best', he's got a 'voice like Burton, face
like Hurt', 'a real drinker', 'cynical',
'upsetting and a real slitter' too,
I'm 'quite a lady' that he'd 'love to meat'.

Dirty and Used

A Foreign Office woman in Berlin
shared her life with a naval officer.
She used to have him tie her to the bed
with the elastic webbing from his kit –
it had more give in it, she said, than rope.

One day, she let out her chief fantasy
was doing it with a wolf, and got him to
put on their shaggy, old, fur fireside rug.

That spelt the end of their relationship,
his friend told me. He moved out all his things
next day, because he felt 'dirty and used'.

Dirty and used? I've never felt that way –
incredulous, annoyed or bored – perhaps. But then,
I've never dressed up in a mat for sex.

Torture

In the New Newgate Calendar I found
the law by which torture was authorised:
'Men are insensible to pain.
Nature has indeed given you
an irresistible self-love
and an unalienable right
of self-preservation; but I
create in you a contrary
sentiment, an heroical hatred
of yourselves. I command you to accuse
yourselves and to declare the truth
amidst the tearing of your flesh,
the dislocation of your bones.'

A mixed-up inquisitorial logic!
What truth did torture ever bring to light?
Victims just aim to please their questioners,
declaring only what *they* want to hear.

These days torture comes with less legal form.
A husband told me that he wouldn't drop
a woman who blacked his eyes regularly.
He'd only want to leave, he said, if she
went off him physically. (How strange to feel
that anyone still fancies you when they
abuse the body they pretend to want,
mark out their territory in blows!)

These fakir-types make their own bed of nails
and lie on it, wear out their lives
stuck with some human ball and chain.

Virtuous Women

Virtuous women are those who do not sell
themselves too cheap or give themselves for free.
In Solomon, the virtuous woman's price
is set far above rubies, we all know.
What kind of rubies though? Idol's-eye-size?
Or just small chips in an engagement ring?

A friend of mine has got this man at work —
her 'sugar daddy'. He saves up for weeks
to take her out for these expensive meals.
'The bill came to ninety-one quid,' she wrote.
'I had the moules marinières — £7.
He got the cheapest thing — the chicken soup
to start.' Next he chose sole while she had duck.
(The rest was gâteau, gin and German wine,
three coffees and two Armagnacs — both hers —
and whisky for the pianist.)

'He wanted me to wear a Twenties' dress,
but I wore armour-plated corduroy . . .
He's very unattractive with bad teeth
and pitted cheeks and greasy hair, you see.
He used to grope a lot, but since I fell
in love' (with someone else) 'he's stopped . . . Now he
tries the odd furtive touch on my bare skin
with his cold hands.'

Poor man, I thought. I read the letter out
to Mum. (She loves to live vicariously.)
'The evil pig,' she said. 'You'd think that she'd
have given him something for his ninety quid.'

Underground

Commuters, a dull lot, all of them —
they're like a party without booze — strangers,
too pissed off to speak to one another.
They read the few ads opposite their seat,
then settle to a paper or their own
reflection in the glass.

The standing ones communicate by touch,
taking advantage of the train's swaying
to stick their erections on your shoulder,
or brush the backs of hands across your cunt;
then exit quickly through the closing doors,
fearing reprisal or response.

Chocolate Blancmange

Some of the ushers at the Old Vic, where
I worked each evening, were American —
students of drama at RADA, LAMDA,
Central. Unlike their British friends, they sat
and talked of stardom — how they'd change their names
to hit the public's fancy, combine those
of cities, stars and states. A greedy one
(quite a nice bum, distorted by packets
of sandwiches stuffed down his jeans — he liked
to eat them between meals in the Gents' loo)
once sidled up as I was selling ice-creams,
told me I was 'a foxy lady' and
his favourite fantasy (would I oblige?),
was licking chocolate pudding, warm and sweet,
off women's breasts.

Out of pure female malice, I just let
him talk and sounded him for details of
what brand he'd use, was Brown and Polson's best,
who'd make it and worse still, who'd clear it up,
could I have cushions on the table top,
et cetera . . . Later, I heard he'd tried
this spiel on every woman there — I came
but third, after the barmaid from the Stalls.
I don't know if he'll make it, have his name —
Rhett Harvard? Dallas Wayne? Manhattan York? —
in lights on Broadway or in Hollywood
and own jacuzzis filled with dark blancmange.

Knickers

My Scottish uncle brought a Greek girl's pants
from Alexandria after the War.

While searching bags for bombs at the Old Vic
(how I enjoyed the fact that well-groomed girls
had purses quite as sluttish as my own),
I rifled through a knicker-snatcher's hold-all –
twelve pairs at least. 'My wife's,' he said and blushed.

When I was ten, a boy offered ten bob
to see my pants. I gave him a quick look
for free. It didn't seem a lot to ask.
My mother'd told me, too, that it was low
to be afraid to show your underwear.

Two art school friends stayed in my place to mind
my cat at the weekend. The guy confessed
to me, 'Her knickers make me horny.'
One time, she left a greyish, washed-out pair
behind the bed.

I can't sense what pull pants have on a man,
any old ones, not just silk and lace sets –
the Alexandrian bags, the pairs off lines,
the navy gym-knickers, my friend's grey briefs –
all covers for the real thing.

Baby Doll

My cousin sent a baby doll for me –
hairless and clammy, waxen yellowish-grey
with sunken pale blue eyes and a mouth pursed
for pouring water in so it came out
through a small aperture between its legs.

I called it Peter – though it had no prick –
it looked too ugly for a girl, I thought.
I used to fill it up and souse my lap.
Sometimes I'd press its squashy latex head
to force the liquid out at higher speed,
yellowing the pee by adding mustard in,
or making diarrhoea with chocolate milk.
Sometimes it vomited and pissed at once.

At last, my mother took my toy away –
afraid I'd show it to some visitor.
Several days later, it was back again,
seated amongst my other dolls and bears.
She'd used half an old shoe dye on his face,
giving him hair and beard, and togged him out
with a sharp suit of black and white checked tweed.
'Peter's grown up,' she said. 'Adults don't wet
themselves.'

His lips looked red against his blue-black beard.
You can do anything at any age,
I thought. I filled him up again. He peed,
marking his breeches with a yellow stain.

Evolution

'Some men are very wicked!' my Gran said
while looking at a monkey in the zoo.
His spectacles of flesh and blue behind
reminded her of someone she once knew.

Carnal Conversation

'Now I was really raped,' a fat man said
to his fat friend walking through the Old Town
in Hastings, the day of the Carnival.
'And I mean *really* raped,' he said. 'Last night.'

They stopped and he said it again outside
the little joke shop that sells 3-cupped bras
marked 'For the woman who has everything'
beside false lips and 'Sexy Cucumbers' –
these obviously unscrew for batteries –
small packs of fart powder and 'Mucky Pups'.

Well, maybe he was telling the world the truth –
if she was big enough to drag him off
and knock him down, undo his zip and fall
on the erection he just happened to have.

Dildoes

Dildoes – they come in varied size and shape –
five foot, five six, six foot, fair, middling, dark.

Is it too much to ask for brains as well
as balls? OK, I've had my share of thrills –
the times when everything's well choreographed –
I put my glass down as we start to kiss;
nothing is spilt; our fastenings all undo
and everything comes off; our heights match well;
I fit him like a glove.

Yet I feel trapped in some dark sci-fi film –
my task, it seems, is sussing robots out.
They look so human it's quite hard to tell
until the things go on about their cars
or use the same set piece to chat you up.
(The one part they can't simulate's the mind.)

Some leave the works in a half-programmed state –
these are the easiest ones to spot – I saw
a cheap Italian model in South Ken,
'Disco?' it went, then, 'Whisky – vodka – rum –
bacardi – coke?' and, 'Fucky-fucky in hotel?'
'No thanks!' I said. Its batteries ran down.

I think I'm still a virgin mentally –
I'm thirty-one, I've had no *real* man.
I'd like to, though, just for the novelty.

Losing Your Virginity

Losing virginity in books by men
sounds like some nasty Stone Age ritual –
bedfuls of blood and screams of pain. It makes
the fuckers feel important, I suppose.

These days, virginity's no sacrifice.
Most girls are technically deflowered
quite young, by tampons or a sudden sneeze,
or just don't realise that something's gone.
When we're grown up, we've nothing left to lose
but inexperience.

My first man didn't notice he was first –
he was too busy telling me what women like.
I might have been *his* first. I couldn't tell.
I was too busy acting more experienced.

Back home, I viewed my image in the glass –
the knowing smile, the womanly evil look –
I hadn't changed. (I rather thought I would
have done.) I could go down to breakfast, still
Mummy's and Daddy's little girl.

Trying Too Hard

The fruiterer's son, just old enough to drive,
lined their chrome yellow Citroën with fur.
He stuck it neatly in there piece by piece.
I saw him at it at weekends, lying
half in, half out, high on the smell of glue.

And there was dear old 'Twinkletoes' who lived
just opposite our house in Creffield Road.
He exercised hard for a month – trying
to touch his toes and cycling in the air –
getting in training for some girl. For hours
before she came he moved the furniture,
subdued the cushions, music and the lights,
then gave himself an even closer shave.

We've all laughed ourselves sick at men like these.
Less obviously funny are the types
who fiddle with your fasteners hopelessly
like drunks at night getting a door undone,
who blow in your ear in January,
forgetting that all Nature's doing the same,
who pay over-efficient attention
to your nipples as if they're nuts and bolts
which, once unscrewed, will make you fall apart.

I question the sincerity of lust
that lacks an elementary competence.
Religion's out and fornication's in.
It's fashionable to score. Men must oblige
and overdo us like their aftershave,
patching together their self-images –
a fur-lined car, a body kept in shape,
gnomes on the lawn, a woman in their beds.
Only their clumsiness hints at the truth.

Nature's Call

A flaccid flasher can get off in court
by pleading Nature's call, a policeman told
me once. 'He's had it though, if caught erect.'

The Law upholds Man's right to urinate.
Gents, unlike Ladies, usually aren't closed
during night hours. Men are the leakier sex.
It must be so — they're always telling me
they're off to pee — a sort of verbal flash,
I think.

Married Men

These married men . . .

The average, straight, uncomplicated type
shifts his ring over to the right, pops round
the corner in a pub to use the phone,
tells her he's doing overtime again,
tells you he'd gone to pee.

Others like to lie *solely* to themselves —
get you to ring, or press you to their cheek
so they can tell their wives quite truthfully:
'I never kissed her, she kissed me. In fact,
she did it several times.'

The candid take you back to meet their worse
or better halves, take the Director's chair,
set up an ad lib drama in the home.

Sadism

Foreplay exists in sadism as in sex —
the early warning signs of cruelty —
the playful slaps that fall a bit too hard.

We all know, or know of, a battered wife.
One I had pointed out to me was slim,
pretty, red-haired, doing small parts in films.
She openly admitted she got hit.
Others I've seen with a cut lip, black eye
or swollen wrists. 'The washing-line,' they say,
'Just snapped . . .' 'I slipped on some wet leaves . . .'
'I walked into a door . . .' They're all on pills.

We all say, when we're young, that we'll walk out
of a relationship if struck. (Perhaps,
those wives all said that too.) It's hard to know
just where to draw the line with subtler blows
and verbal sadists who inform you first
before they have it off with someone else,
or men who specialise in 'accidents'.
(These last catch rings or cuff-links in your hair,
rest their full weight, kneel on your legs in bed;
their hard 'caresses' leave you bruised.)

Weddings

One of next door's Scottish relatives got
Maggie's Sarah and Tony's Anthony
playing at Weddings on the lawn. Sarah
gave Anthony half her bouquet of weeds.
'He doesn't get flowers, he's a man!' the woman
said in scorn. Sarah looked hurt.

I never played that game. I hate the chance
it gives to bourgeois sods to plan your life
in His and Hers. (Why shouldn't a bloke have flowers?)
Besides, I've seen too many real weddings.
I used to sing at them in my church choir.
We'd belt out 'Jesu Joy' for half-a-crown.
Once we got less. (God, how we loathed that bride!)
A fat man sang 'You by my side' instead.

Transpersonal Psychology

I was asked to a fancy-dress party
held at the home of a psychologist
on Friday the thirteenth.

I waited all done up in Twenties' style.
Alan (in undertakerish top hat
and tails) turned up seventy-five minutes late
to take me there. I made a mental note
to ditch him in revenge, and visualised
myself leaving with some more glamorous bloke.

The analyst greeted us in the hall,
a paper bird mask on his head, held on
with a blue dish-cloth hanging down the back.
It fell off every time he bent. His wife
stood by, a rabbit in her arms. (I'd met
him once before – Alan had told me then
that he was teaching him some martial art.
They'd disappeared into his studio
and made a lot of grunts and thumps.)

The Living Room had 'Hag Bags' spread around.
These have a girl's face printed on the front
with holes for eyes. (I sometimes wonder why
people don't shove their bodies into sacks
and let their heads hang out instead.)

I sipped some wine and played a little game
of Spot the Patient with myself. Those who
went up and hugged the plump psychologist
had to be mad – transference and all that.
Others, with any luck, might be all right.
I looked at them – a tart, a female judge
wearing a satin curtain and a half
(too orange to be red, with rufflette round the edge),

a nightied girl singing in a cracked bass
(made *Summertime* sound more like Wintertime),
two Satanists, a witch, a hippie or two
and several masks.

The only tall, dark, almost handsome bloke
was insecure. 'Hullo, I'm Mike,' it said,
and shook my hand a dozen times or so,
and then apologised *two* dozen times
for being drunk on gin. I edged away
to read the noticeboard behind the nuts –
lists for *Transpersonal Psychology*
and badges of all types – *Gay Whales Against
Racism*, *Stick-Insect-Owners* CND.
'The Hastings intelligentsia's here tonight!'
a man whispered. He probably was right.

Soon after that the food arrived.
Some of us sat down on the floor to eat.
'His rabbit makes its toilet down behind
that sofa in our group,' a woman warned.
My martial arts friend sat down awkwardly.
(He wasn't as fit as you'd expect, or else
his trousers were too tight.) He kicked my wine
over and wandered off, leaving me by the stain.
It seemed a timely cue to go and pee.

The first-floor loo was in restful sage green.
The door, I noted with relief, would lock.
(I've heard stories about encounter groups.)
There were booklets for constipated types –
Starship Snoopers, *One Hundred Irish Jokes*.
White toilet paper flowed from Thatcher's mouth.

A wide bald bloke had followed me upstairs.
'Is anyone inside?' he bawled outside.
I thought a bit, then answered, 'Yes.'

Impotence

A man in his late thirties told me once
he'd kill himself before he reached old age
and couldn't manage sex.

I said that there were other things in life –
things that could leave more of a mark behind.
Painting the Sistine Chapel didn't appeal.

He was the adolescent-groper type –
the sort that doesn't try for any more.
One date and he was off – to give this spiel
(presumably) to someone else.

I've had much the same talk with other men.
I wonder how they'd know just when to die.
Do they allow themselves a second chance
after they've failed to come on cue *one* time?
(An ageing prima donna often has
many a 'last performance' with encores.)

I've never known a man be impotent
with me – well, not for more than five minutes.
I sometimes wonder how I'd handle it –
is it humiliating for the girl,
or only for the man? – I hope
that I'd be kind.

The truly impotent, I think, are those
who do not even try in case they fail.

Headaches

Men are the ones that have the headaches now.
Back in my mother's day, when girls said no
most of the time, they were all after it –
or *so* they said – in pain with their erections.
But now we call their bluff by answering yes –
the truth is out – they want it less than us.

Most of my female friends are on the pill,
willing, good-looking too. What do we get?
Men who can't *quite* make up their tiny minds.
The bastards are all Marvell's-mistress-coy,
perhaps insane, certainly undersexed.
What *can* the problem be? Are they afraid
of pregnancy or rape? Or is it just
that men fear sex is like a driving test
where they must get every bit right or fail?

Two men fell laughing through our chemist's door.
One said he'd like some pills, something to give
his friend. 'What's wrong?' the chemist asked the man.
'He hasn't had a girl at all for weeks.'
'That's normal, sir!' Too right it is, I thought.

Respect

A girl who'd lectured me on how to keep
a man's respect – she had a code of what
to touch and when: this week the lips, next week
the breasts, the rest verboten – got married
to a pig farmer in Norway. (I heard
this at an Old Girls' evening over quiche.)

My body's no cliffhanger serial –
I don't want men to leave off till next week
once things get to a tantalising point.
(Most by-instalment books in magazines
give you a cheated feeling by the end.
They'd gripped you only by suspense not style.)

I want respect of quite another sort –
for men to see my feelings are as strong
as theirs, my aims the same.

Second Choice

Some men don't think affairs are worth the fares,
or even the price of a long-distance call –
say 20p cheap rate, out of peak hours –
to summon you to meet them.

A girl I know was dropped when her job went.
She worked close by but lived nearly an hour
away by train. Her man then reasoned I
might do – I'm near – just a mile's walk for him.
No need, of course, to ring me up before.

Last time he came, I hung around upstairs
and peeped between the attic banisters.
(I'd recognised his legs through our front door,
reflected in the mirror on the stairs.)

He knocked and knocked, ten minutes in the snow . . .

Morning After

The morning after and there's little left
for either one of you to say.

There's nothing in his rooms. (The coffee that
he'd asked you back to have was never there.)
There's only time enough for him to drive
you into work – his place not yours.

He swears at every passing motorist
along the way, before he stops to put
you down. 'Last night,' he says, 'was . . . interesting.'

And you're left standing there. You notice then
he's dropped you far from where you'd meant to go.

Post Mortem

I got chatting to a plain-clothes policeman
on a Newmarket train. 'We're not much like
Starsky and Hutch,' he said. 'We often talk
about it at the Yard. We've decided
we're more *The Sweeney* than *The Professionals*,
and I'm a sort of Regan type – they had
me up for rough stuff, just like him. *I* was
just cautioned.'

Then he went on to tell his flasher tales.
('We let the WPCs handle them . . .')
Next, all the corpses he had found –
stinking old ladies lying in bed-sits full
of jumble clothes and memorabilia,
the milk accruing on the steps outside.

Good, jokey stuff – he'd told the lot before,
that was obvious. I half thought he'd strung
together bits from all those TV shows,
until an admission of weakness . . .

'My first post mortem, trying to keep out
that smell I used half a tube of Polos
and soaked my hanky in 4711.
It's all right if you go prepared.'

Doctors' Kids

'A man sat on a cucumber, he said,
while phoning in the nude, and came to get
the thing extracted . . .' 'A womb dropped out,
pulled by the vacuum of a milk bottle . . .'
'A pair of farmworkers went for advice.
They'd learned by watching birds and bees perform,
mistaken the act, and now came asking why
they couldn't get a child however hard
they tried . . .'

Doctors' kids tell a special brand of tale –
they pick them up like things their parents treat.

Flashers

Poor Clifford haunted Creffield Road until
they caught him on the bridge in his beige mac.
He said his wife was pregnant at the time.
The magistrate was touched. The fine was small.

Some others, like ill-kempt commissionaires,
or lions before the Palace Beautiful,
do sentry duty, picket loos or schools.
I saw one too, by Nero's Golden House.

One half of the 'nice young couple' who took
the top converted flat across the way,
nightly at twelve stands naked in the back
while flashing blue light strobes him by the glass.

I've got a bit blasé, less nervous now,
each time I see some bloke grope for his pin –
they always use the kilt or nappy type
to keep their trousers closed – zips can get stuck.

But I hate those who come behind you in
some lampless street. You're unaware until
a splat alerts you to their presence there.

The Ladies' Oracle

One year I found *The Ladies' Oracle*
in my stocking. A Victorian reprint,
the cover showed a fat-faced girl in red,
holding a fan across her chest. Inside,
there were a hundred questions to be asked:
'Is his heart as affectionate as mine?'
'Ought I to fear the tête-à-tête?' 'The gentleman
that I am so glad to see, what does he think
of me?'

There was much in that book's vocabulary
that struck me as odd, even then. I scoffed
as I tried all the oracles. (The men
I knew weren't 'gentlemen'.)

Years on, I've found some kinds of people still
use Ladies'-Oracle-type words, ask if
I'm 'courting' – (a comment on my lifestyle?) –
or, like the fat woman opposite, rush round
to tell us how some girl a block away
had paid her shabby bed-sit's weekly rent
with 'certain favours'.

Milk Round

Our old milkman was ginger and sun-raddled
and specialised in Freudian shouts: 'I've just
got sterilised today,' 'Those wretched tits
have poked the gold tops in.' For several months
we had to go and buy milk in the road.
(The woman who'd owned our place before,
he said, had once inveigled him to be
her acolyte in funny rituals.)
Glandular fever forced him to retire.
He walks his young Jack Russell by the sea.

Then came a succession of younger ones —
all erratic. Some days they never called.
'Well, I was drunk, wasn't I?'

The next one was addicted to Yorkies
and miniature pork pies.

Two old ones do the round together now.
They give each other drinks from a thermos.
The milk seldom comes till the afternoon.
They leave details of their various offers —
you can pay by the week for a hamper
of wine or a seven-pound selection box
to arrive next Christmas, or get manure
delivered to your doorstep from their cows.

Charity

Our school was very hot on charity,
its Scripture Room was always stuffed with knits
and poison-lilac bath-salts screwed in jars.
(My Alma Mater had adopted some
Korean orphans and each autumn term
held the 'Korean Sale' in aid of them.
Their mission sent a photo every year –
they all had specs and western-christian frocks.
The ambassador's daughter once came too,
to thank us all on their behalf. She was
the only other Korean we had seen
and looked a little different in chic silk.)

At eight, we made small candleholders out
of clay. Our teacher took us to a hut
beside the emptied swimming bath, where the
caretaker used to hang his uprooted
tomato plants to ripen in the showers.
(His small green fruit never seemed to make it
past yellow.) Our fingers bleached and crinkled
rolling grey balls on boards muddied with slip.
We who were only used to the homely
hot-cats'-piles aroma of plasticine
smelt mortality lodged under our nails.

The years passed in weekly donations, sales
and Harvest Festivals of windfalls for
the hospitals, bonked tins for Acton's Old.
And 'Dorcas' when we made tiny garments
with large needles and larger hands. Each form
did a lurid layette for the Third World –
a lemon orlon matinée jacket,
pink shawl, blue dress and bri-nylon bootees . . .

I went along with it until the Sixth,
when greater action was required. Most thought
I was a shit for opting out, but yet,
I couldn't take the thought of forcibly
redecorating flats in my own choice
of colour scheme for frightened OAPs,
or giving Christmas gifts in Old Folks' homes
of pencils taped to soap made by The Blind.

Giant Hogweed

My teacher, wholemeal-faced and nature-crazed,
brought wings into our fish-tank classroom just
to show their workings – she'd no sense of smell.
A friend had sent her them by parcel post –
a pigeon's, sparrows' and a kingfisher's.
(It seemed all wrong that halcyon feathers
should stink as much as any city bird's.)
One hot week on, the wings just had to go.

I tried to look for things to brighten up
the school and put my weekend's fungi in
our bath – I thought to keep them fresh.
Broad Dryad's Saddle, Cep with its bun top,
the mealy-warted Blusher bruising pink,
a Shaggy Ink-Cap like a lawyer's wig,
Tawny Grisettes and Beef-Steak Fungus from
an oak, all turned to slime by Monday's light.

Later, a Giant Hogweed caught my eye –
at eight, I loathed the catkins good kids brought.
Miss Davies, too, never believed my tales –
the bullfinch was a chaffinch on my tree,
the raven but a carrion crow. As for
the carpet-wetting wallaby I saw
at Christmas in the Lyric Theatre –
'Well, really!'

My sci-fi weed had a cool reception.
(I'd lugged it on the 207 bus,
its seven-foot stalk trailing across the seats,
my father held the end, I had the flower.)
A show-off's bloom, too tall, too poisonous,
no fit companion for the sensible
contents of a nature table. They stood
it in the corner by itself.

Worms

The good kids in the class read *Look and Learn*
and were encouraged to experiment
with insect life. Santa always brought them
encyclopedias. They all admired
the School's tape-worm in gin. (I wasn't good –
I stayed away the day the teacher'd said
she'd show that jar. I made my parents write
a note that ran: 'Fiona has a cold . . .')

I cut a worm in half once with my spade,
egged on by Mum in Education's cause.
I wasn't amazed the thing went squirming on,
just sickened by my obedient cruelty.
'Fuck Science!' I thought. 'I'm sticking to the Arts.'

The pen is kinder than the knife –
what it dissects still stays intact.

Flannel

When I was ten we had a special book
for Needlework — some pages ruled, some plain.
You wrote up how to do a stitch on ruled,
then cut a window in the plain and placed
your sample in behind and Copydexed
that page down to the next.

One day Miss Smith brought us red flannel in —
two bits per girl — one small, one minuscule.
We cut our own hole in the bigger piece
and herring-boned the smaller square on top,
then wrote 'How to Patch Flannel' in our books.

I half remembered from Victorian slush
I'd read, flannel was given to the Poor —
shirts for the honest, broken working-men,
petticoats for their honest, broken wives.
Recipients all had to be Temperance
(typhus, consumption, cholera also helped
you qualify). So where did we fit in?

None of my class had seen the stuff before.
(A flannel was a nasty bit of towel
some people scrubbed their faces with, most thought.
Boring relations gave us them as gifts
with soap leaves in a plastic toilet bag.
Once used, they soon acquired a mouldy smell.)

Gwendoline Smith died several months ago.
The Old Girls' twice yearly news sheet carried
its usual paean of praise for those who'd gone.
She'd set off for the Holy Land, it said, one year
(she taught RK as well as Needlework)
with bedroom slippers on. Miss Smith and friend —

another Scripture teacher from the School –
taxied to Harrods en route for Heathrow
to buy a pair of shoes. They caught the plane
with seconds left to spare.

Yours Faithfully

'Carols' at Haberdashers' Aske's involved
a lot of suffering. You had to learn
the lot and stand there singing them for hours.
Our teachers made us smallest kids recite
in class weekly throughout the autumn term,
and yelled at us if we forgot a line,
or even had a vague look in our eyes
as if we didn't quite remember things.

We had to stand in perfect graded rows –
Serve and Obey, the motto of our school –
chests out and stomachs in and rubber soles,
shifting to make a gangway at the end.
A hairy gym teacher hauled fainters out.
Miss Watts conducted us. I liked to watch
her fleshy arms wallow and jump
beneath black chiffon sleeves.

My first faint, I was eight. Matron put me
to bed and went back in to see the rest.
The Sick Room smelt of Dettol and felt hot
from two electric fires. It only had
some spattered, battered Blytons on the shelves.
The bright red blankets made me itch. I slipped
my gym shoes on and went off home.

I had to write apologies next day.
(Matron had feared I'd turned delirious
and wandered off, they said.) Like Hell she did!
I wasn't daft enough to swallow that –
I knew that they'd just found another thing
to get me for. (She could have rung my home
to ask if she'd cared tuppence how I was.)

My teacher stood and watched me as I wrote.
'Put "Yours sincerely" at the end,' she said.
I didn't feel the slightest bit sincere.
I hated her, the School and Matron too.
I put "Yours faithfully" instead.

The Great Clean Up

Late summer term – time for the Degree Show –
all but the last-year students must migrate
library-ward, giving place to let their
Augean studios be transmogrified.
A heavy-duty cleaning team descend
to terminate the Jackson-Pollocked floor.
The battle's lost – islands of grey lino
emerging through a chloracne of oil
and acrylic. Next, Jake the black porter,
smiling, rides a great grey dodgem into
the corners. Swirling, pulsating brushes
throw a delicate dirt-spray – mist rising –
air-brush painted, four inches up the walls.
Partitions are screwed and unscrewed, and old
angles reveal a morphewed umbrella,
gummed brushes, part of a piano. A
sink's walled up, algae-green, festering with
full years of brush-wipings, exhaling a

heady gripe of white spirit. It's our turn
now. We get going on the old walls and
new whitewood subdivisions, hold roaring,
wrist-breaking orbital sanders against
lumps and irregularities, firing
out streams of sparks. All old nail holes are filled
as we begin to eradicate the
last owner of our private wall, every
smear and pencil mark is resented. Then
a sporty slap-slapping of emulsion
brushes and our work's begun. The walls are
enamelled white, coat upon coat. Soon I
retire, snow-blind, to the well-graffitoed
comfort of the Ladies to read such gems
(illustrated) as 'Don't drop matches down
the pan – crabs can pole-vault.' Our studios
turned gallery seem sterile as we hang
our pictures – dead exhibits – minus notes,
sketches, explanations, clutter, shifting
them critically, polyfillaing
our old holes. All's done – the end of a phase –
the place emulsioned older like our hair.
Downstairs, life ticks on in the Print Room. The
black iron presses roll; proofs emerge from blankets;
an etcher bends, his hands immersed, head in
the fume chamber, his fag-ash drops in the
nitric acid; files scream on bevelled zinc;
a flutter of pale yellow resin melts
on a copper landscape.

Bird Man

Sculptors come in two types. Some like to gouge
or chisel images in wood and stone,
others build likenesses in wax or clay,
then cast or fire to get the end result.

Thirteen or fourteen years ago, I went
to evening classes in an Ealing school.
Some of my lot were regulars. One man
carved a small penguin out of wood,
wearing it down, each night, each term for years,
seeking to make the quintessential bird.
(He said he'd cut a Virgin out of stone
before, but liked the softer feel of wood.)

His wife was in the next class painting flowers.
She'd come by at the end to take him home.
Small, old and frail, she hardly spoke a word.
(He'd cracked two or three of her ribs, he said,
in giving her a hug.)

The night he finished working on his bird,
he threw it at the teacher's head. The beak
snapped off. He couldn't find the chip to stick
back on, so started carving it again,
next evening in some other person's class,
paring the penguin's body down to fit
its broken head. The rest of us
just stuck to modelling in clay.

Private Parts

Pencil is less ambiguous than paint,
incising hard lines round the genitals.
I've seen art students, broad-minded enough
to talk naturally to naked models
in their breaks from posing, become furtive
as they draw a penis – men too. Often,
like children cheating in exams, one hand
shielded the other's workings from all view.
Others erased madly – they'd made it far
too short or long, then found they'd worked
the paper to a grubby thinness there,
or left black rubber pills like pubic lice.

Marble's cold and doesn't change however hard
you stare at it – an easier task than flesh
to draw. Sketching a Roman Mercury
in the Fitzwilliam, I'd toyed with the thighs
for far too long, eyed by some soldier
from a US base nearby. He stood until
I gravitated to the balls, then pounced.
An ugly human, he'd identified
with the smooth body of a god, the image
on the paper, seeing my pencil's touch
as a caress.

Still Life

The Ecole des Beaux Arts makes students do
traditional still lifes of game, I'm told.
A sad American who studied there
had two of my art school friends to stay with him.
His days were spent in painting meat or fish –
a brace of pheasants rotting on a plate,
some salmon caught three months or more ago.
Each evening he'd return depressed, back to
the vicious, childish, French girl he lived with.
(He felt responsible for her, he said.)

My friends – do as the locals do – tried horse,
tried to ignore the rows around the flat,
tried to ignore the sad American
when he came in their room at dawn to draw
small conté sketches of whatever bits
of them weren't covered by the sheets.

Memories of Pantycelyn

My mother, back in nineteen thirty-five,
went on a bicentenary coach tour
of spots from the Methodist Revival,
persuaded by her distant relative,
Annie Davies, who, though a pagan type,
trampling her grapes for wine and rearing goats,
gloried in a mutual descent
from William Williams, poet, hymn-writer.
Llandeilo, Llandovery, Pantycelyn . . .
The coach stopped at his farmhouse and they all
trooped in. The Visitors' Book lay open
at the signatures of Lloyd George and wife.
On leaving, A.D. plucked an ivy leaf.
'Olive,' she said, bristling with pride, 'now press
this in your Bible, so you won't forget.'

Later, they stopped to see the chair *he* used
brought to a humble cottage door
by its inheritrix. One by one, as I did
with a commode in Osborne House,
having a Queen Victoria fixation at six,
thirty sat down and tried the thing for size,
stared solemnly imagining him write.
(When inspiration struck in the small hours,
his wife would have to bring a candle in.
Now since I can't progress past Lesson Ten
in Teach Yourself, I do not know how good
his Welsh work is. His English hymns aren't bad,
though one has 'My corruption' as refrain.)

My mother, frequently sick on buses,
shunned food and drink along the way, until
she, weakening, took ice-cream at Lampeter.
Later, she leant against a wheel and striped

her hands with oil. She'd lost her hanky,
so she used the leaf. 'I once had hopes of you!'
poor Mrs Davies said.

Cockroaches

The Stalls crowd eating salmon at the bar
suspected nothing of the teeming mass,
a cast of thousands underneath the fridge
that held their ices for the interval –
their chocolate, strawberry and vanilla tubs.
One night, some careless usher dropped his change;
we had to move the thing to get it up.
Out came the cockroaches, big, little, large,
by ones and twos at first, dazed by the lights,
they straggled on. Then came a seething crowd –
returning veterans from Waterloo.
We left the room, lacking the killer drive.
The crackling-creaking-rustling quickly stopped.
They'd all returned to their ancestral home.

In time, some trendy so-and-so decreed
(ignoring the past visits of the Thames),
the basement decor needed livening up.
He had it done in smart brown hessian
to show off theatre prints – costume designs
from plays – grey aluminium-framed, for sale.
The Thirties' paintwork was all covered up,
and things got warmer. He'd not bargained for
the insects having his same sense of taste –
brown sacking – just what any roach would love.
They did too. What a Spring they had – up, down
and round about – they even did things by
the cloackroom hatch, rode on velvet jackets,
drowned in gin.

58

'A Touch of Class'

'I wish my husband were more romantic,'
a woman complained to me. 'He's nice-looking,
but has no imagination at all.
Now I'd love to have tea in the Churchill
like Glenda Jackson in *A Touch of Class*,
but *he* just wouldn't think of things like that.
You know, if I could find some other man
to take me there, I'd go with him instead.'

I often wonder if they ever went –
husband and wife, or wife and other man.
Probably not. I reckon she just bought
a video of the film and sat him down
and made him watch it all a hundred times,
hoping he'd take the hint.

The Drinking Club

We have become the victims poets abuse,
Neither a writing equal nor a muse.
Good men will always feel the better for
Dealing in psychopathic metaphor.
I am reminded of an Arab guy
(My singing teacher's lodger some time by)
Who, after kissing, spat upon the floor –
It was religious fervour, nothing more.
Poets do not kiss and tell, but kiss and spit,
Slashing our faces with their Ripper wit.
An aged writer slangs his ageing wife,
Mocks her cardy, sticks in the verbal knife.
You'd think the fuckers might show gratitude,
Not take a Christian-Father attitude
Of cold contempt. Each video-nasty lyric
Becomes more pornographic than satiric.
Misogynists should stick to masturbation,
Not make us, dead or injured, inspiration.

Our work must be a social-worker's verse,
A-plus in caring, technique D or worse –
For editors will fit us into roles
Before they place us in their pigeon-holes.
Nurse, Arvon Lady, mother, wife or witch,

We must not suffer from ambition's itch,
Our husbands may though, and if we are able,
They'll let us write upon the kitchen table.

Senility and cancer are two themes
Most prevalent in women's verse it seems.
Pox, constipation, herpes are all out,
Brain-fever's too old-fashioned, so is gout.
The Arvon Ladies' samples win the prizes,
Foundation-packeted in handy sizes—
They're all organic (that's grown in shit or such),
Free from impurities, which can't leave much.
Some write short pieces on domestic bliss,
Stanzas on ironing clothes and such-like piss.
Mentions of breasts (but never boobs or tits),
The moon and menstrual blood are frequent hits
With those who like a girl with occult powers
Who sits and plays with tarot cards for hours.

Thus, editors by every wrong selection
Dismiss us all as the inferior section—
Under-achievers, low-paid workers too,
Branded inferior in what we do.
The literary world's a drinking club for men
And females aren't invited to that den
Where macho-boys with beards boast of their feats
With alcohol or screwing in the streets.
Our presence there might represent the truth,
And show their exploits up as just uncouth.

The Obscene Kiss

Arse-licking literati lionise
stray moggies at their Sabbats. But I fear
that tuppenny-halfpenny Fausts get small reward.
Hundred advance? A good review or two?
These devils' pockets are not lined with gold,
and souls, like sparrows, fetch a lousy price.
Yes, they will fly tonight! Tomorrow finds
the riches dust. Cold treachery! I'll not
stoop courtier-wise to kiss. That's not my path.
This tongue (descendant on my Welsh side of
three hundred years of preachers' tongues)
can't shape itself to anilingual exercise.

The Muse

'I write poems too,' a man said to me,
'at least, I used to, before my Muse left.'
(I was eating mince-pies to drown the taste
of plonk at a small Christmas private view.)
'I used to just stand up and let it flow,'
he said. 'I didn't *really* write them down.'
Muses and gods get blamed for everything.

I have to work at poems, draft after draft.
Some days are good. Others are bad –
when I'm too cold, too tired to do things easily.
(Women, of course, don't have the wherewithal
to please the Muse – we all know that from Graves.
So I *can't* be authentically inspired.)
I should be a White-Goddess-substitute
for some male poet – get off my pedestal
only to make his nourishing snacks and cups
of tea – and not presume to write myself.

I think, *if* there's a Muse – if *I* were she –
I wouldn't like those men who claim to speak
my words when they are only using theirs.
I wouldn't want groupies who looked like Graves.